Bearing the Juice of It All

poems by

Nancy Lynée Woo

Finishing Line Press
Georgetown, Kentucky

Bearing the Juice of It All

Copyright © 2016 by Nancy Lynée Woo
ISBN 978-1-63534-028-0 First Edition
All rights reserved under International and Pan-American Copyright Conventions.
No part of this book may be reproduced in any manner whatsoever without written permission from the publisher, except in the case of brief quotations embodied in critical articles and reviews.

ACKNOWLEDGMENTS

Grateful acknowledgment to the editors of the publications in which versions of these poems first appeared:

"Lament for a Skin (Ode to a Selkie)" / *San Gabriel Valley Poetry Quarterly*
"Bearing the Juice of It All" / *Breakwater Review*
"Thunder, Lightning" / *Synaesthesia Magazine*
"The Relinquish" / *Cadence Collective*
"Ode to the End of the World" / *Synaesthesia Magazine*
"Love in the Fourth Paradigm" / *The Camel Saloon*
"Blues and Greens" / *Cease, Cows*
"New Mexico Sea" / *Artemis Journal*
"Postcard…" / *Breakwater Review*
"The Rescue" / *Penwheel Lit*
"War" / *Confrontation Magazine*

Publisher: Leah Maines

Editor: Christen Kincaid

Cover Art: Kelli Woo

Author Photo: Mick Victor

Cover Design: Elizabeth Maines

Printed in the USA on acid-free paper.
Order online: www.finishinglinepress.com
also available on amazon.com

Author inquiries and mail orders:
Finishing Line Press
P. O. Box 1626
Georgetown, Kentucky 40324
U. S. A.

Table of Contents

Hooks 1
Lament for a Skin (Ode to a Selkie) 2
Professor of Bees 3
I watch my mother run away from me. 4
Perhaps the hardest thing… 6
War 7
Bearing the Juice of It All 8
"The Drama of the Gifted Child" 11
Thunder, Lightning 13
While Paul Simon Plays 14
The Relinquish 15
Ode to the End of the World 17
A Woman Alone 18
Dinner Party 20
Blues and Greens 22
Valentine's Day, Chicken Heart 23
Postcard to my future lover, who will be my lover for a while, and then disappear again into the wilderness 25
After Having Loved Wrongly For A Whole Decade 26
intertidal zones 28
Sunday Aubade 30
The Rescue 31
All of It 32

*For all my girlfriends underwater
and for those who have found dry land*

Hooks

The apology burns in the crater
of my chest, scraping to get out—
prized fish wriggling on your line.

Unraveling, skilled at clutching
tightly, apologizing, sorry sorry *sorry*
thin bones resolved to bear it until—
twisting on wire, my silver guts
slowly spill about your non-
                              waiting.

Sorry years to unfurl goodbye
heated, aglow, in orbit and I
whiplash love affair, green-eyed
what's missing here?
tight ball releasing into wind.

Please don't make me
a fool again

Let me hook in you
only one tiny pair of words
and my pulse with them.

I'm still holding the line, ready
to throw myself at you
lose myself in you again
            or return to the glitter of the sea.

Lament for a Skin (Ode to a Selkie)

Salt flurry of wind rush
the boy running to his mother
        breathless—
this one moment agape forever.

Eyes like the crest of a wave
sea foam locks
heart stricken for the blue
        she sees what he holds.

Slick black skin, pelt shining
damp of seal—

she grabs it and the music plays.
        Doesn't even ask
where he found it
but kisses him tightly, yelling
for the others, sun-beaten arms
closing around them like a lid.

Quick, hard love and she
turns to release the door,
as blown about as
        the western wind.

Honey legs tumbling down
to shore, pillow of dress
sloughing off to sand,
        she catches
sight of a man, shadowy
in the distant green,
        stopping
as his fishing pole drops
toward a gallop.

But she is already at the sea
glistening joy of ocean mist
        and her hands are already gone
        and her legs are kicking into fin
        and her lips are whiskering away
as the light plays upon the waves

and she calls to her children, goodbye.

Professor of Bees
After Sylvia Plath

If all women are whores
the coins that jingle in her pockets
milk the tender of humanity

Infants appear out of nowhere
thrown down on the bed
all golden and bloody

Big flopping wings
a shriek
in a manor

And that one ghost wind that creeps
around the curb of the heart
muck-sewage vibrating in the veins

A great vacillating drum, brown
and sticky in the parlor of the street
where the people *lean*

Blue hair and ringlets
large green doorways
a meaty, summer chill

A chain-link watch
kissing and doorbells
they glow dim

Under some complacent moon
swept up in a silver tide
jump

Where the skirt hitches
live bright, frightened women all bees
buzzing in a jar

What does it feel like underneath
that hat?
I know your children

would not have said go.

I watch my mother run away from me.

I watch my mother run away from me. Red hair
swishing, a well-trained pony's backside but
I cannot hear the whip as she paces around the track.

I watch my mother run toward me, arms a pair
of torpedoes set to fire—I am old enough to know
I am not the target as she turns the bend and

I watch my mother run away from me, reliable
fan of her feet carrying her away from something
I am too young to comprehend, black soles

of her shoes two snakes constantly nipping
at her underfoot—the rattle of my father's
shout, the hiss of my grandmother's wail,

still a cloud around her as she runs, kicking
up more dust, a wave of red that picks me up,
pummels and drowns, teaching me tornado.

I watch my mother run toward me, her 5000th
lap, the boom of her feet hitting soft clay,
a boom I echo and repeat, echo and repeat.

I watch my mother run away from me,
but running, at least, preferable to those days
immobile, sneakers like neglected children.

I watch my mother run toward me, as if
carrying a messenger bag from the capital
to the village—shouting, *They are coming!*

But she couldn't shout. She could only run
in circles. I watch my mother run away
from me, pungent glow, marathon of ache

poring out of her—that I could see. I watch
my mother run toward me, her muscles taut
canons locked and ready. I watch my mother

run away from me, blur until she disappears into the mirror of the sand, mirage leaning into a finish line, always just up ahead.

Perhaps the hardest thing…
After Anne Carson

Perhaps the hardest thing about living
with an abuser is the way your throat becomes
gradually shackled, dog rope greening
at the neck, and him tugging at you
to smile. It was her—not me, but the whole
time I felt his push and shove, wild rhino
thunder of his breath an all-consuming yellow.
That day when he had her choking
on the ground and I heard her bluebird cries
I flew and my voice moused a halt at him,
her broken fence of fear and his slow advance
I found myself between. Menace of eyewhites,
dragging hoarding her in his den, whistle
of lies tightening as she faltered.

Perhaps the hardest thing about locking
his bullhead out was not her wind of tears,
but how she snarled at the sky and wound
herself back up to him, deep red marks
a hurricane he fitted her for, blind cavities
of warp deepening to rot and scream, wild
bruise of her jaw bared at anyone who tried
to sneak her free, so we reached a *must
let her go*, watch her dive into his turbulence
—and him, how he stood there, vortex
of need and grimace, like a gun cocked
and heavy, how he still stands there,
right outside the door while we sleep,
pacing back and forth, waiting
for her to let him back in.

War

We are all attracted
to a soldier or a suicide.
Watch out

for a sweet tooth. I once heard
a woman could tell when she
was not seeing clearly

but thought she was. It might have
been a rumor. The bear is always
on the hunt, except

when hibernating. She walks
to the well to grab water. We see
her jug on her head.

We see her coarse black hair.
A cat's whisker is nothing
if not a lifeline. Soldiers

or suicides. Clean feet
a sign of civility. Someone
always dies. Inevitability cannot be

tragic. Enjoy the warm
bath while you can. And the shells.
And the birds. Especially the trees

and the children. Let your guard
down once in a while. Forget even
what this is about.

Bearing the Juice of It All

                9.

She—or rather, the ancient She—
wanted to drink in the honey
like a funnel from the gods
but it was too sweet for tasting
without becoming a junkie.

She wanted to crack,
a coconut ripe to be split.

Fast forward to the end,
she raced forward to the end
and it wasn't   pretty

                8.

              It was beautiful.

Bearing the juice of it all:

A frightening ripeness
that squirms to be let out
and though She wanted
to nurse the idea

Get back in, we said.

                7.

How does any She-beast
              react when caged?

She rages—with a furious
reason that boils all things
down   to the quick

                6.

              The quick.

How quickly a cell divides,
even while building
foundations for a house
brick by brick.

She has a reason for being
other than igniting now.
But words   cry

              wrongly

            5.

All She can do is dwell
in the courtyards of the blaze
and wait for the thirst to dull,
give way to more than vapors.

Wait, the sign on the gate reads.
In her womb is only the word.

            4.

She wants to grow things,
move molehills into mountains
and bring kittens milk.

Not destroy.

            3.

Biologically addictive, we have
                no antidote
save murder, religion and the third eye.

            2.

Unsatisfied on a bed of dead roses.
Tiny figurines of fertility, of stone.
        Pins   and needles.
No more unpenned cancers

riding out into the wind.

The time will come.

1.

Our bodies lay motionless—
I want a sturdy home built
on reason making love to faith
and we have enough of neither.

When we emerge, She is quiet
and the waiting room stretches
longer than the labor of love.

"The Drama of the Gifted Child"

> *Therefore it is necessary today for the individual to find [her] support within [her]self, if [s]he is not to become the victim of various interests and ideologies...*
> —Alice Miller, psychologist, 1981

I couldn't be a mother at 18. He'd be six now
(I know it would have been a boy, kind of like how
at the moment of conception I knew it had
happened, though my mind said *maybe it didn't*
the sweet intelligence of the body always knows).
The father would be bald and defeated, still
working the 4 AM shift at the drive-thru
Starbucks, fuming in smallness and we all
would have turned caffeinated and mean.

I wouldn't have had time to discover the life
of this pulsing bereft. I'd turn cigarette helpless
and wine bottle drunk, turning away from my heart,
accusing the baby of killing it. So it wasn't a decision,
just like the breakthrough of the zygote wasn't
anything more than a repercussion. And it wasn't
as hard as you'd think, more like evacuation
than murder. My body grew this vine. My body
can cut it. Strange bundle of cells from my body.
My body wouldn't have yet learned love. My body
was mine before it was never his.

A friend of a friend brings her two-year-old over
and we play. Crayons and counting, she is so smart
with mixed eyes and fat cheeks, I adore her
with distant womb love, so much I would never
give her a mother with only one arm to hold her,
the other aching for more, how my mother cradled us
idly. My little lips kissing ghost flesh while she slept.

I didn't mind sinking $500 into the evacuation
after Baldy refused to take responsibility
for his moaning part in the play because I know.
I know when my mind and body are in sync
I will paste myself into the right here right
now and make macaroni noodle masterpieces
all day long because I will have spent years

creating space for the growing personhood
of my child to breathe. My body will feed him
only after I have grown into full-self. I'll know
so he'll know. He'll know without any
phantom ache his mama is okay, is full-body.
He'll know his mama can do anything, did
everything to love him right.

"The Drama of the Gifted Child" receives its name from a book with the same title by Alice Miller.

Thunder, Lightning

It's rained for the past three hundred days and I'm beginning to wonder if the sun has abandoned us. Favorite red boots have a hole in them so these two feet have been stalling in mornings. I stomp in the barn. Clouds milling over cows. Looking out the window into my own barren white. The earth I see has two suns on opposite poles, one for growing and one for loving under. I would rather the brighter one. Swampbeds attract leeches. I am pulled toward the tension. Perhaps it will be this night forever. I have been dancing with fireflies and filling canteens with a star's distant murmur, as it calms one's thirst. The cool water sighs down my spine, twirling me through winter's heat. Small blue fire speaking in licks, I wait for the light to slip through the cracks again. What we wanted all along was peeping bright but we've been cooking in darkness this whole dreary year. Icicles form on the tips of tongues slit. Firing, warming, scorching, steaming: hearth stories break apart limbs when we tell them. Either combust or erupt, how long this wait is. Are we reaching higher out or just cupping the lid? The bed knows, but the sheets have stopped speaking to each other. Frozen over. The fire is enemy, warm enough to forget the only way out. Afraid of the squelch. To get out from underneath this horrid rain, one must squish the boots asunder, feel the worms in between the toes, and take a good look at the sinking cabin. Meat rotting in the basement. Flies hatching. Webs surround us. It was all new once, and now it is night. Shades drawn. Homes do not last forever, even on sacred ground. Like all animals, get up, lift your seat, simply carry your weight away.

While Paul Simon Plays

We danced and I thought
we were really dancing. He moved
his hips and I shook. Pushed
up against the wall, we sang. I said
no but didn't mean it. He said yes
but didn't mean it. His words
were shifty, eyes looking up
and to the left, lidded with secret
nails—crayons, rope and wanting
to cut open. I don't know
if it was him or me who first
unlocked the snare but once inside
the record player warbled
and the doors shrunk down
to false exits. I cannot tell you
I escaped—he'd simply worn me
to a nub and the first graceful
thing he did, he shoved me out.
Even now, I marvel at how I had
been convinced we were dancing—
bulky movements shadowed
by a string, a wooden cross attached
to every move. The music played,
but we were not in love. Not quite
scientist, I dove in to that dark
region that spread like fever-chills
across the map of his mind
to discover something like evil
drew us together, and pulled
the curtains closed.

The Relinquish

No longer are you the invigorate
or the titillate
of my exalt

I must do the dump of the dishwater
and remove the cherish
from my nightstand

clean out your linger and sulk,
scrub down your rouse and chafe.

Deep hold of hesitate.

The dreams grow thicker
with my linger
though like every sour savor

I wake with tongue heavy,
pockmarked.

How can I get out from underneath
your elevate?

Haughty sticks around a fire,
I throw it all into the languish.

Is it my mind, my misguided
arteries pumping or my swollen
skin that needs you

to narrate how my cells squirm?
Do I exist in my body
or yours?

Underground of the resist, I follow
the ethered string that links us
to the crevice where I keep my agonize—

it is hard and yellow, and
smells of sulfur, a deep recess where
nothing but slime is born,
but I remember.

I remember when I thought
surrender would be a palace.

Ode to the End of the World

From here I cannot but peek. From whence we came... no, for whence we... Whence we say the word whence what synapses wince. Forever pickling I peek. My steel water carrier leaks. John fetch a new comb! My hair. Oil. Wanting to be sleek. Roses are red. Roses are... roaches not as many here—the stink greater. How babbling rivers speak, now that they have putrified I see. Out into the air—I peek. From where? We came from another hill. Now, caskets of damp wood: our sleep. From babies to mothers. Rags. I can't remember the blood but taste metal. The narrator peeks. Looking through a tiny hole. Through the woods we go... to grandmother's house we... someone mop up the blood, please. It is slippery here. I have always known this was coming. Melancholia in the well water. Cupping and spooning it. What is it? A pronoun is a handkerchief of no determined pattern. I used to grab roses to catch nosebleeds in the forest. Here I can't see the forest for... Do you remember trees? All we have is this crate and the musk of the end. When language dies, we go with it, muddy and celestial and everything I see I have only peeked. So I sing. We are too tiny to be sad about this to be or not to be. I heard one time a wise pig say... *Hakuna Ma...* When life gives you... what is it? Lemons he she we be. It! Give peace a... whence. Live and let... yourself to me. Rosewater. The roaches are enormous and dead on their backs. Our words much smaller. Are they more alive? I wanted peace. Or a piece of it. The barn here is rust. Metallic on the tongue. Something needs a deep, fortified cleaning. It's the happiest... no, the merriest... no, the dustiest place on earth, here where we can see, and see that we have only peeked.

A Woman Alone

A woman alone is seething
with secrets too shameful to share
ideas of littleness, her bright head
more a balloon than a light bulb.

Her flesh, a disguise adapted
for entrapment, more
a carnivorous plant
than a free wheel roving.

A woman alone is at first
suckling at the dried up
teat of love, questioning
whether she is even there at all
or just a ball juggled in some hands.

It is the shame of being a vessel
but a vessel that can feel shame
that funnels history into her chambers.

A woman alone is bountiful
in her uselessness, feeding nobody.
She has no need for jealousy's mirrors,
doesn't want a man cave. She has the luxury
of time. She begins to read in between
her own lines, worry less if she is pretty.
What she has to offer is beautiful.

A woman alone meets the mothers
of revolutions who radiate foundation,
their names faded with their youth, absent
from history books, but their strength
present, clear, connective, a rope.
There never was anything to prove.

A woman alone is rumbling and rolling
in the agony of her own birth. She looks up
to see her mother's hand clasping hers tightly,
her sister's, her grandmother's, her daughter's.
Pregnant with understanding, she peeks

above her chamber, catching glimpses
of others peeking, too—

Rooms upon rooms of other women
scratching at themselves and staring
back at her, wide-eyed, surprised to see
an army awakening from slumber.
Winking at each other, turning to hug
the ones they love.

A woman awakened is industrious.
She grows rose gardens on paper,
lets the smell of baked pies waft
through pen strokes, mends clothes
of dirty, faded ink and dons the armor
of someone who accepts she may need it
as she steps deeper into the stream.

A woman alone is not a gaping void
but a fierce general of a global family.

A woman alone is not a shell
desperate to be filled—
she is the open container in which
new beauty of thought, succulent,
has always had the audacity to grow.

Dinner Party

Circling on tile like a Russian ballet,
burner off, cork popped, sauce stirred.
Grab the glasses! someone says. Flurry
of feet carpet over stacks of stuff
to set the table. Rustle of wings.
Bring out the cheese and bread!

We caw out of our mighty bellies
the birdsong of survival, as we
pour the red, check the oven,
toss the salad. Hummingbird wings
beat over 1,200 times per minute.
Five ladies here spinning two plates
per palm, at least.

Don't drop the rolls, but grab
the butter. Don't drop the keys
to the apartment, but let us all in.
Don't drop the memos. Don't drop
your beauty regimen. Don't drop
your family time. Don't drop
the cleaning, the bills, career.
Careful, your relationship smells
like it's burning. Check the temperature.
Put back in, or let cool. Don't drop
your future. Don't drop. Don't drop.
Don't be exhausted.

But balance your self-love at the center
of your gravity. Don't drop out
on your girlfriends who remind you
to salt and pepper. Just clink
the bubbly. Sit back and split open
the cheesecake. Don't think about
the gym later. Dive in, fork to lips.
Let it all out! As one rinses. One suds.
One dries. One wipes. One tidies.

We've built a good team.
The production value of this dinner
skyrockets. Meander back to couch,
soft hugs when needed, tough love
when the time's right. Always clinking.
Erupt, we each get to be Vesuvius—
and for a moment, set our plates down.

Blues and Greens

We speak of the most intimate barbs in low growls. Chicken wire poking out of my throat, blue today but going back to green, there is a tiny laughing Buddha jumping on my chest. Sometimes, he is only an angler fish and I have swum too deep. No women allowed here. Back to the top. Where the grass seeds sprout, the raccoon with smoky eye make-up digs. She is looking for the eggs thrown from the Easter basket. Sustenance from the rising. Vanished. When I am quiet, all I am is gratitude, a resonant electric blue, though the rest patters against the windshield, I try to take the curves with grace. My mother's love is a refrigerator, nearly empty. A sick green. But she read to me. She planted my bellyhead with words enough to hate her then forgive her. A hate so full of solitude all I could do was will it blue, caress it there, let all the little growls scare back at the fish. The light dangles but I am clear mist over only my own grave. One hand reaching for the shovel. Always only one—I will not be that hungry. I will wait, and I will float back up. What left to do but when Friday comes, buy a ukulele and strum nonsense on out into the sea until I have anchored in my grip, until I am that balloon drifting out from hand, and I am hand, and feet, and grass. From here, one rubber band all the colors of my spine holding things together, I can almost taste the order of the sky—just enough to devour it all and begin again.

Valentine's Day, Chicken Heart

> *I want to know some things for certain, and other things for vague.*
> —Ada Limón

Tiny once-beating thing,
so specific. I know now
for certain how the rubber salt
of heart tastes with wine.

It is still vague what mine
is doing. Let's not even begin
to confuse me about yours.

I know some things for certain.
Like the length of the yakitori
stick—8 inches—and the distance
between my doorstep and yours—
467 miles. I am certain of this:

It was 128 days we lived wholly
separate lives in between,
and only 30 seconds to touch.

I am certain you are more
concerned with the impersonal
language of zeros and ones
than tropes about chicken heart.

Our languages meet at odd
angles—in small doses. Small bites
of flesh on scraps of wood is all
we can swallow of each other.

I know how chicken my heart is,
how yours calculates.
I am certain I don't know when
I'll be seeing you again.

But I do know how once I froze,
my heart clawing at wire
in panic at your lust,

a fire I could not name.
We both felt it when
I left my body, limbs
feathering out and away
from the warmth of covers.

I was afraid: This is certain.

But it was not at all vague
how you held me, nearly a stranger,
cooed me back with grace.

A man uninterested
in keeping me small.

Neither of us know whether
we will ever meet again,

but it is as certain as blood
how I put my heart on a skewer
and you tasted it,
washed it down,
stroked my hair,
went to sleep,
woke up,
apologized,
gave it back
bigger than you found it.

Postcard to my future lover, who will be my lover for a while, and then disappear again into the wilderness

Already, we are returning to that house in the woods. You look over to make sure I am dry, but I grew gills long ago. There are men standing above us when we arrive, thinking they are repairing the roof. You do the things you are supposed to do. Unlock the door (all the windows are already open). Grab my hand (like it is already yours). We step gingerly across the mat of succulents and moss booming out of the floorboards. Oh my. The pufferfish is large today. I don't ask you to kill it. Only tell me which part of its bloated body you admire most, which spikes you relate to. As you can see by now, the fish tank is everywhere. We look up and tap the boots of the workers as their rubber heels bump us. Don't worry, we'll make room for you, I say. I'll explain the best I can why the faucets work so well. I'll offer an old umbrella, in case you like that sort of thing. Cook soup. Thick flesh of salmon. Mosquitoes fight over the bones. Watch out, there are hooks everywhere. These men think they are repairing the roof. But light still gleams in from the surface, glinting off blurry countertops. Whatever you do, don't try to convince me there is no rust in these cabinets. Just seek out the best sort of oxidizer and I'll get started on the humidity—and the tiger sharks—and the ghosts.

After Having Loved Wrongly For A Whole Decade

The colicky, mushroomed ground
has swallowed me up before, shifting
cavernous rock widening, Cheshire cats
and fruit flies emerging from the rumble,
sewer rats and blue-breasted butterflies
spilling across every torrid corner of earth—
only every person who has ever been
helplessly in love knows
what kind of quake this is.

It is a dumb awakening underfoot.
And then you go. A weightless drop
down
     down
          down
into a broken compass of black.
Little Alice plummeting away,
skirt billowing, eyes all amiss
cupping one hand over mouth,
life suddenly tilted, exploding
into a deck of hearts, games
with no rules, wrong-sized tears,
chasing—chasing after a rodent
in a sharp vest.

Eons spent dungeon-crawling, trying
to remember a way out, flashes
in the dark, big teeth, grinning and lost—
      how you fear it could always be.

Then one day, after an era inching
blindly on knees, forcing cracks open
here, dragging skins forward
there, finally a knob and   *whoosh*

      this part so bookend fresh
        its pages are all blank—
The hourglass shifts, the winds start
blowing gustier than the vacuum
and little Alice finds herself

shooting out the other end of the tunnel
as the northern lights.

You are *his* Northern Lights
and you have never been so
        supernatural—
so wild honey, so smeared masterpiece
so easily good. Years of rabbit hole fever
seconds ticking to madness, and now
you're floating on brilliant doorways
at the edge of aurora borealis—
        escaped and stupidly happy.

How does one survive this sort of thing—
the surviving after spending years down there?

I can only turn to caterpillars for answers.
Listen to their wise quiet. As old skins
shimmer, bloom and fade away.

intertidal zones

> *Few organisms can survive*
> *such harsh conditions.*
> —Wikipedia: Tide pool

the spit of rocks wide around us
peripheral noise of barnacle waves
world crashing at husks

I am at the beach   with you

wrenching, I stir in my nacre
splash of white, tough hangers-on
they are stuck to me

the tricky musk of purple
prickling on their claws
grappling at my face

let me kiss you
let me pet you
let me pummel you

they, always jutting out, grubby
like eels their fingers
swooping to devour

cragged touch
let me win all of you
salt gulping, hair flowing

from afar, a sea caw
your hands in the briny air
do not pry

but the suction pulls at my bodice
      these anemone
           tendrils of men
      half underwater living

am I stuck again?
am I small again?
they are always sea hunting

I can't see your net?
am I caught in it?
won over, a prize, I glitter

they rush at me as you stand
        at the lip of it, and I become
golden sun and coral light

breaking bone, unhiding
        I lunge off
calcium splinter, mollusk free

from above, silver blue mist
        around the edge
                of everything

I touch   your face
        panorama
ample room for a spin

side-stuck to clouds this time
feet stretching to sea
I will not crawl back inside

I plunge my face into the water
see you eye smiling
I am up bubbling

I am dew
I am rock
I am eager, unhinged, refitted

I am tide drunk from loving you
and they—their spindly suckers
they float, recede, duck under

they, they, they—

are slowly disappearing
a fog attached to a dream
erosion on our lips

Sunday Aubade

Sunday mornings are my favorite thing
about you. A fullness so exact, we

must shut the blinds. Your hand,
my stomach. Precisely. Boxy,

a settling into, like the moment
at a restaurant after ordering, a sigh.

That particular pleasure of knowing
what is coming. It is the settling I love,

into coffee and blankets, slow TV.
Your delirious summer eyes the perfect

opposite of rent due soon and the check
somewhere in the mail. I think you will not

surprise me with absence. Slow pan out,
we see: two animals warming each other.

The quiet lick of safety. Protection
from the hunt, a predictable

nesting. Bored and not tired of it.
After all the running and the running,

we are so vividly aware of rest,
allowing ourselves to pause

and simply hold each other. Humans,
loving easily, how difficult the trek has been.

The Rescue

A hound dog howls
by the side of the road.
I used to know that song
that wishes loudly for a peopled fire
and biscuits, soft touch.
Tail wagging as I approach
with my gun, I realize
those long dying days are done.
I call him into the bed of my truck
and feed him scraps of night
until we're both full.

At home, the medicine cabinet
is nearly empty and pups
are due soon. The sky blooms
after storm and a hot plate
waits in a cozy kitchen. Out back,
my bloodhound sniffs at dandelions,
back leg scratching, paws busy with bone.
But as I watch, leaning from window
in between load of dish and towel
in his eyes do I spy a glimmer,
a slight murmur and pause,
do I catch him remembering
the long dark he came from?

All of It

Cold-toed midnight. Blanket-wrapped, I worm to the right to be closer.
Hip fitting here, shoulder snug there, limbs pretzeling over, under
breath wavering, I hesitate to say out loud, these honeysung words:

> I've never had *this* before.

Lazy-lidded, you question what I mean by *this*.

Safe-haven sails immediately open. Near-dawn sea storm crashes around you,
your dry land. I attempt to decipher this. Murmuring bees in the jar of my heart.
I strain to overhear their conversations:

> What do we fear this time?

Worry-hornets. Buzzing and stinging at my ribcage, nearly frosted over.
Squirming for answers to the question of your nearness. I open my mouth.
And let one bee-thing out. You catch it with your tongue, and swallow. Easy.

Again. One at a time. Slowly. Mountain moving. Effortlessly catching
one, after the other, as they sneak out my teeth: *flick, flick, flick.*
The hive is hushed by your appetite. Our good geometry.

A baby stinger in my answer, I try again:

> I've never had *this*.   All of it.

You respond in quiet and sturdy beekeeper's tones. A buoy
to my cloudburst. Hands smoothing over. Wrapping your wide
comfort around the shore of me. You steer and bob us

toward horizon, drifting off into sleep—
Fretting. Calmed. Your arms. Around me.
The unmistakable sound   of time
                                            in your voice when you say:

> How   do you know   this is all of it?

Thank You

Many thanks to the writing communities who have lent their eyes and ears to these poems: Eric Morago's workshop at Half Off Books, Danielle Mitchell and The Poetry Lab, Cadence Collective readings at Gatsby Books. Many thanks to PEN Center USA for giving me the opportunity to grow as a writer through the Emerging Voices fellowship. I am very lucky to be a part of so many wonderful writing communities.

Special thanks to the fine editors Terry Ann Wright, Alejandro Duarte and Eric Morago for helping this chapbook reach its final form.

My ladies of the women's circle—Holly, Heidi, Elmast, Raquel, April, Candace—we are sisters-in-arms! (Maddie and Tasha, too.) And Long Beach salon friends, every last one of you—we keep each other inspired and I love you so!

Deep gratitude to my friends and family who unconditionally and robustly support my poetic efforts, including but not limited to: my dad Robert Woo, my mother Carol Ludlam, my godfather Gary Reissman, poetry warrior-goddess Tina Matuchniak, creative co-conspirator Alex Hattick and soul sister Holly Carpenter. Thank you sister Kelli Woo for the beautiful cover art.

Nancy Lynée Woo is a 2015 PEN Center USA Emerging Voices Fellow, and co-founder and editor of a social justice-focused literary press called Lucid Moose Lit. She has been published with *NAILED Magazine*, *Artemis Journal*, *The Subterranean Quarterly* and *Cease, Cows*, among others, and has released a chapbook, *Rampant* (Sadie Girl Press, 2014), and a poetry-music CD, *Face the Blaze* (Blacksheep Music Productions, 2014). She received her bachelor's degree in sociology from UC Santa Cruz, and currently resides in Long Beach, California. Find her online at nancylyneewoo.com.

www.ingramcontent.com/pod-product-compliance
Lightning Source LLC
LaVergne TN
LVHW050045090426
835510LV00043B/3189